.

THE HOOD WITH NO ENGINE UNDERNEATH

Terrance Vidaud
Ceetle2nd

OVER THE WORLD

Inland Plug LLC
First printing, 2020.
ISBN: 978-0-578-71909-2

OVER THE WORLD MANAGEMENT LLC.
WWW.OVERTHEWORLD.US

Table of Contents

THE HOOD WITH NO ENGINE UNDERNEATH

Introduction

Play The Game For What It's Worth

"There are five important things for living a successful and fulfilling life: never stop dreaming, never stop believing, never give up, never stop trying, and never stop learning."

— *Roy Bennett*

Such an awe-inspiring quote, isn't it? Full of meaning. But it seems easier said than done. Never to stop dreaming, believing, trying, and never to give up. However, this is the key to success, especially learning. Our life is turbulent. Yes, there's no denying. Still, achieving a successful flight is possible. To spread our wings and take off in the direction of our dreams is possible and achievable.

You must be wondering what makes me say this with such affirmation. Well, my life's journey up till now seems to be going by this quote. No, I did not abide by these marvelous words of Roy Bennet. I never gave up or stopped believing in myself either. My dear reader, by now, you must be curious about my identity and why I am writing all of this, right? Well, allow me to introduce myself. I am Terrance Vidaud. I currently reside in Rialto, California, 45 minutes east of Los Angeles, but my life was not always the way it is now. I endured endless storms and weathered my way out from near destruction to safety.

Having grown up in the inner city, my life was on and off subject to lesser opportunities due to racial discrimination, not having profound resources, being blocked by obstacles that would just pop out of the blues, lacking proper guidance, and so much more. One can even say that I lost more of my energy when times were rough, yet I surfaced through all of it. I emerged stronger, brighter, lighter, and content, given perseverance, and not giving up. To simply put it, I was just another youth growing up in a ghetto community where we do not have the best of assets, we need to start a life. I still held on dearly to my dream. A dream of being an entrepreneur, being self-sufficient, and reliant.

Today, I proudly claim to be the CEO of *Over the World*. An organization focusing on branding and entertainment. This rendered me the opportunity to work for some renowned names of our industry today. Back when I was just a teenager who had no door to knock on for help, I was a victim of low morale. The only thing that kept me going was my will and determination - my self-belief.

Today, I want to share this with any individual, youth or adult, whoever seeks to embark on the journey of entrepreneurship solo. Trust me, if you dream of starting something by yourself, if you believe you have the potential, then you have it all to take your first step. From there, your journey to success will not be a breeze. You will reap the benefits that you will sow in the form of determination and hard work along your way.

Having successfully diverted all the negative forces in the form of hindrances, I am triumphant. Through this book, I aim to pass on my strengths to you. Through this book, I assure you that you will be able to source your energy and motivation that is at the moment hidden deep in your soul. Through this book, I aim to extract your hidden potential and surrender it in your grasp, to mold as per your need and use it as your guiding light to fulfill all your dreams. Now all of this may sound dreamy. Words you might have heard before too. But I will share with you my techniques, so prepare yourself to stand on your feet and walk toward your success.

"If you can't fly, then run. If you can't run, then walk. If you can't walk, then crawl. But whatever you do, you have to keep moving forward."

– Martin Luther King Jr.

Chapter One

Hood Dreamer

Importance Of Defining Your Goals

Ask yourself if your daily goals bring you closer to your main goal. If not, wouldn't you want the things in your life to change? If you look at the lives of the world's most successful people from different walks of life, you will notice they have one thing in common – defining goals. It is an important part of their success. Now, the process of defining goals is not one-size-fits-all. It is unique to your life's vision.

The importance of defining goals cannot be stressed enough. Goals are essential for your development in personal and professional life. They create a road map for success. They give a definite starting point and a clear destination to reach. The list of benefits is almost never ending. Thus, you must stay committed to overcome challenges and work toward achieving your goals. You must stick to the discipline required for achieving the set goals in your life.

It is always dark before dawn, but have you ever noticed the approach of dawn every day? It is very methodical. There is an order for every day. First, it begins with the warmth and energy the sun provides us with. It gets us working and moving. Slowly, the day starts to set, taking us toward a pause. This is when we wind up our work and head back home to relax. Why? Because the day has drained us of energy and we need to replenish ourselves for the next day, which we do by sleeping at night. We go through this order daily but fail to identify the pattern and induce it in our goals. Everything needs an order to go about seamlessly and with minimum disruption.

If we implement this ideology in everything we do, imagine the endless success we can achieve. So, how can we do this in our daily life? By breaking down our dreams and goals, just like how a day is broken down into hours. Break down what you wish to achieve. The more you break down your goals, the smaller and more achievable they will be.

If you look at your dream as a whole, it will be overwhelming because you will be looking at a bigger picture. The journey of an entrepreneur is the same. All you have to do is stop focusing on your dream as a whole and break it down in bits to define the goals you wish to achieve. This will enable you to focus on one thing at a time. It is the practical way of your outcome turning out positive. Now that we have covered the importance of defining your goals, let's make it more feasible for you. You know the importance of defining goals, but how do you identify them in the first place?

Identifying Goals

Do not fret. With a big idea in your head, research into it. It is crucial to do so. This process will help you identify your goals. With research on your idea, you will come across various suggestions. Some of them will stick with you and make you establish what you will be working on first, then second, then third, and so forth.

One of the tried and tested methods of identifying goals is the SMART approach. This is a vital key that you can use to identify your *specific, measurable, achievable, relevant,* and *time-based* goals. To come this far, first you need to write your defined dream. With your big idea written in front of you and the research you do, you will come across all the steps on how to work on it. Start small, write the initial most and the smallest step first. Then write what comes next.

Alas, you have all the steps listed on paper, but when the time comes to follow them, you run out of energy and motivation. What do you do then? It seems there's something you need, something you lack.

Self-Belief

This is one of the most vital parts. This is the essence of achieving everything. This is the key to turning that lock of your dreams. There is no point in knowing your goals, identifying them, and so on, if in the end, you succumb to fears. Fears are always there and are very real. If you know what you want, that's your reality. Why run away from reality when you want to embrace it? Think of your fear in a different way. Your fear makes you realize your true potential because if your entrepreneurial idea is not worth it, you will not be worrying at all. It will not be worth your brain's energy to make you feel nervous.

If you choose to see that the reason you worry and doubt is that your idea is worth your time and efforts, you will choose to believe in yourself. To believe entails the power to swim through oceans. If you believe in your dream, if you believe in yourself, you can achieve your goals. Trust me when I say this, take it from someone who has been in your shoes, someone who had no helping hand, resource, or financial asset, but today that someone runs a successful organization. Had I not believed in myself, I would have given up.

If something makes you worry, if something makes you doubt yourself, it is very much real. Acknowledge your worries, work on them, and continue taking steps forward. Trust your mind, heart, and body, and you will not doubt something if it is not worth it. If something is worth it, you need to tell yourself to do whatever it takes to work for it. The harder something is to achieve, the more it is worth it.

Remember, years of failure lead to success. Tears, sweat, and blood, all are futile if you do not have self-belief. It is the soul of self-worth. Without it, you are just a walking vessel. Your dreams paint your life. Irrespective of your current standing, in spite of the hardship you are facing, if you have a dream, even if it is big and seems like wishful thinking, you are the only one who can bring it to fruition. For that, you need to map out your idea, break it down into hourly bits, and take a second look. You will see that your idea is not impractical and then you will feel it in your heart. You will know that the drumming of your heart is its proclaiming of belief.

It is natural for a man to worry, but if you choose to render yourself a little bit of self-belief, you will see your potential, and this will get you through an amazing journey. So, now if you are ready to know more about how you can achieve your dreams, take a dive into this book, and let it open all the locked doors of your potential...

Chapter 2

Geniuses Still in the Hood

Talking about potential, it is the ability each individual possesses. We are, after all, born with the same brain. Only our mind and mindset differ, affecting our potential to go far in life. Often, unfavorable circumstances come in the way, too, of an already slow process to success, affecting not only us but also the community we are a part of. Sometimes, the case is vice versa.

Now, what do I mean by unfavorable circumstances in the community affecting an individual's success? I simply mean that the lack of opportunities present around one affects many. Such is the case in the ghetto community the most, even in present-day times. Yes, although we deny it as a society, this is the reality of the *hoods*. In present-day times, the biased structure of the community outside the hoods not only drastically affects opportunities but is also depleting access to the community. I am referring to the inner cities where black communities are in the largest number and where young talent is buried even before they get a chance to discover their talent. The youth residing in these ghetto communities do not get a chance to surface. Why? Simply due to the lack of a concrete educational and financial infrastructure. We are living in 2019, where instead of running from the harsh truth of the ghetto community, we need to work toward them to provide them with an equal living opportunity.

We are well-versed with living standards that fall below what any other person would be comfortable with living outside the boundaries of the hoods. Now in such an environment, how can we expect the youth to have a proper nurturing environment? Certainly, the youth are forced to be stuck in the vicious cycle just the same as their adults as they never experience a positive change. Studies are conducted endlessly. Despite all the efforts, no one is able to pinpoint the reason for the failure of the hood.

Why does the ghetto community fail to thrive, no one knows? But if we pause, take a step back, and instead of carrying on with the failed researches that are futile, how about we focus on finding a solution? See, irrespective of the harsh living conditions of the hood, there are endless names that have managed to come out of their low-income living conditions and achieved a successful career. From job-doers to entrepreneurs, both young and the mature, people from the ghetto community do have the potential to change their course of life. This is what I would like to highlight and emphasize for all my readers. There are hidden gems, geniuses stuck in a loop of no-opportunities that can be broken.

The Need For A System That Nurtures The People In The Ghetto

What makes it hard for these people to see their worth then? It is simple, even an undiscovered diamond in the rough is just a piece of coal. It needs someone to work on it, provide it with the right conditions, and polish it to shine to its full potential. In the same manner, the ghetto community needs people to believe in them and render them aid. The hoods need such a system that can enhance their skills and work toward a better future.

In the past and even today, the youth have been exposed to a biased society. Even in the inner cities, wherever the youth go, they find it hard to be employed. To begin with, the schooling system present in the hoods already suffers due to the lack of funds provided to them. As a result, only a handful of students tend to take their studies seriously. The reason for the rest of the students not invested in their education is that they feel it does not secure them a future.

Employers hire either a person with a renowned school certificate or someone from their own ethnicity. Such a biased hiring process is not limited only to upscale jobs but also downscale jobs. In recent years, there has been a rise in the immigration community. Most of these readily open up stores where they prefer to hire their own people. Furthermore, since they have access to flexible loans, such stores pose a threat to the ones owned by the ghetto community.

On the other hand, it is already hard for a black individual to have a successful application for a loan. The reason being the simplest of all that they are unable to provide concrete security to get a loan. But the immigrants can receive a loan from even their own community - loans which are known as risk funds. To elaborate a little on risk funds, it is a grant given on the basis of trust to new entrepreneurs that boosts their morale and allows them with a fund to set up their business with flexible and customized conditions to return the money. Such a loan is inaccessible to the black community.

Due to this very reason, even the existing African American business has paid a hefty cost, resulting in them to shut down. The aftermaths are devastating for the entire community as they witness another shutdown, discouraging new entrepreneurs from risking their savings. Furthermore, the job opportunity a new business could create dissolves, resulting in more unemployment within the hoods. This discourages the youth in the hoods, irrespective of them having the necessary skills to be successful in their endeavors.

Ghetto Life And Lack Of Opportunities

Youth is the future of every community. If their wings are cut off before they get a chance to fly, how will they ever mature into a better and bigger person? To begin with, the education system of inner cities is not as per the standards of most employers there. Due to a lack of subsidies, the youth find it nearly impossible to leave their families behind and venture elsewhere for education. They see their adults suffering unemployment that greatly demotivates them even to believe in hard work.

Lacking opportunities and watching their family slip into the slump of poverty, the youth resort to the easiest most way of having a livelihood. They turn to crimes, of which the common most is selling contraband and narcotics. There is no way to justify crimes, but watching your loved one's sleep on an empty stomach when you have no source of earning, will you not go for the only available employment out there? The answer lies within your heart.

However, this is preventable and can be overturned. The youth of the hoods can work on a better path, only if one is provided to them. At hand, the youth are greatly discouraged by the lack of funds. If more people trust and provide funds inclusive of risk funds, we as a society will be providing hoods with a better tomorrow. If the ghetto community can be trusted, it will provide them with the platform they need. If new entrepreneurs are encouraged, they will create more jobs within their community. Hence, with employment, the youth can be saved from pursuing an illegal method of earning a livelihood.

I myself came from the same background. I had no savings, quality education, or access to a secure job that would pay well. But today, I stand as an entrepreneur who has a stable career. So, take it from someone who has been through an endless struggle. What matters the most is knowing yourself and your inner strengths. I knew myself. I knew I had the potential to change my life for the better. With that belief, I worked hard and relentlessly.

Nobody will show you the way but yourself. So even when your future seems bleak and hard to comprehend, know to hold on. The only way to get out of something, stagnation, or hell as we commonly call it, is to go through it to come out of it. Find new opportunities and knock on doors that are deaf until one opens for you, but just don't stop.

New entrepreneurs will be encouraged to make most of their skills if they are provided with an improving system that believes in them and reinforces them to continue working until they develop a system that will benefit their community. All that is needed is a little belief by fund providers who can provide the youth of the hoods with flexible loans. The capital injected into the ghetto youth will be a nudge that they will need before they start the walk of their life.

Left: Terrance Vidaud
Right: Iddris Sandu

Chapter 3

Youth Identity

"Older men declare war. But it is the youth that must fight and die."

— *Herbert Hoover*

Life has been stuck in a vicious loop, where the lust for power and dominance often leads to wars. These wars come with a hefty cost of a merciless massacre, hunger, poverty, and endless brutality. But who truly suffers the consequences? It is the youth that suffers and survives through the aftermath of such destruction. Time and time again, humanity has faced a similar fate, but we fail to realize our mistakes and learn from them. We fail to understand that our youth is the essence of our future.

There will be a time when our bones will grow old and will no longer be able to carry the burden of ourselves, let alone the burden of this world. We surely cannot let the world tumble down then. We will be relying on someone else, someone younger and full of zest, life, and energy to carry on. That someone will be the child on the street who is exposed to a hazardous life. They are the key to unlocking the world that lies ahead. They are the seedlings who require proper nurturing to grow than to be uprooted or fed poison.

Let me ask you, are we dealing with our youth in the right manner? Take a second and think over this question, because if you think the answer is positive, then you are wrong. No. we have been dealing with our youth in the wrong manner. Instead of nurturing them properly, we are crippling them with our own hands. And how so? By preaching pride and ego, by showing them a set of life through our actions that is filled with negativity, we are teaching them to follow in the footsteps of ignorance instead of teaching them how to stand up and help another one stand back on their feet if they are down.

Having grown up in a ghetto community, this is one practice that I see engraved in the minds of our progeny. Let's take a look at what I mean.

The Ghetto Mentality And Its Effects In African American Communities

What is the Ghetto Mentality? Simply put, it's a result of an environment where individuals are living a stagnated life with substandard living conditions because they belong to low-income families. Despite us living in 2019, African Americans are exposed to racial discrimination and socially segregated from even their own kind. So much so, those who make out of the *hoods* do not turn back to offer a helping hand when they have the opportunity.

As a result of having faced endless discrimination for more than 40 years, black people are far comfortable in the lives they have constructed for themselves. Irrespective of finding it hard to make end meets, the zone these African American families create for themselves is their home, which they never wish to leave even for good reasons.

Their lifestyle, as often perceived, comprise the stereotypes of the hoods. The environment is often such where a promising talent of an individual is crushed just to cope with the expectations of their community. Having been exposed to poverty and abuse for a long time now, African-Americans are accustomed to a life of pain and suffering. The constant need to protect themselves from abuse has made them far more vulnerable than they admit. Because of this vulnerability and fear for safeguarding themselves, they find it difficult to be interdependent on someone from outside their circle.

Having constantly been fighting in the hoods and the streets, the majority of black people are short-tempered. They often don't shy away from raising hands on the weaker ones to assert dominance. Come to think of it, who doesn't like the feel of power? What these people fail to realize, however, is that they are setting a negative example for their children to follow. Growing in an environment where children constantly see their elders abusing one another, where families fall apart because of the normalized consumption of alcohol and drugs on a day-to-day basis, leaves an indelible impression on young and naïve minds. Sadly, that's all a black child in the hoods thinks there is to life.

The youth in the hoods are brought up in an environment where they only hear people address each other with negative endearment. Folks are degraded when they see someone committing a crime. If they dare to snitch, they are threatened to be outcasted from their community.

Often, these people do not have sufficient money to escape or seek shelter somewhere else. Also, thugs are treated better than someone who wants to do a regular job. It is already hard for a person from the hoods to get equal opportunities as someone else, and when they do, their own community doesn't allow them to break the community norms for good.

The Need To Break Norms In Ghetto Communities

Children, these days, are smarter than we comprehend because they are always paying attention, even to the trivial-most details. You might have come across your child catching onto something quicker than you could have thought. Why? Because by nature, children are inquisitive and curious. To them, this world is a place to explore and discover things. They believe people around them are fascinating.

So, what happens when they are exposed to a life of abuse and bigotry? They follow the same footsteps.

Life in the hoods is already agonizing due to a lack of opportunities. With no proper education, it is hard to get out of that life. But exposing the future generations to a lifestyle in which drugs are normalized and the selling of narcotics is valued should not be encouraged.

Change is crucial to have a better lifestyle. No one wants their children to lead a life of dread. So, know that the power to change lies in your hands. You have the power to let your child have a better future, even if you do not have the means for it. If the youth of the ghetto community are shown how their adults are willing to step out of their comfort zone, they too can take a step forward. Because at hand, the youth are only following in the shadows of what their adults do. A little encouragement from you can give the youth the opportunity they need to change their life for the better. But how? Let's dive into that now.

Changing The Ghetto Mindset

It is hard to leave the life you have seen growing up and then living it by yourself. But it is even harder to imagine your child to be facing the same discrimination and suffering as you did. Only you cannot push the younglings to lead a life they are unaware of. It is an instinct for a person to reciprocate the actions they are used to.

Nonetheless, you should not be rigid to change. If you want to achieve something for yourself, then take your first step. Seek counseling when the need arises. No, there is no shame in consulting a professional to help you overcome your fears. Start small, by giving respect first when addressing someone. Do not talk in a condescending manner or a negative tone, especially when you are around someone younger than you.

Most importantly, look up at those who were once from your community but now stand at a better platform. Learn from them. Because if one person has successfully walked out of a life of hardships, so can you. Make patience your virtue and believe in yourself. The day you will start trusting yourself, you will continue to push past the walls you have built around yourself that are resistant to change.

Our youth have the power to move mountains. I believe in them. Their talent is hidden due to the *Ghetto Mindset* we adhere to. But is the lifestyle worth our youth losing opportunities daily? No.

In conclusion to this chapter, I would say yes, the ghetto mindset is hazardous. We do not have to be constantly hostile. We do not have to fight the world when we can initiate peace. We need to understand that dominance is not everything in life, but happiness and simplicity are. If we continue to set a bad example for our youth, they will never live a happy life, let alone see their skills and talents and put them to good use.

If our youth remains blinded, needless to say, the future will suffer. If we continue to teach our youth to be aggressive and short-tempered instead of instilling patience into them, they won't be able to work for a better tomorrow. Instead, they will create an environment of violence and abuse, continuing to be a part of the same vicious cycle they grew up in, unable to rise above themselves.

Chapter 4

Social Trap on the Mindset

What are the social traps? They are a devised yet an unspoken scheme of the society that lures a person's mind into doing something. One may call it society's manipulation, whereby an individual feels liable to do a certain thing for a temporary social gain. Irrespective of the temporary gain not being of use in the long run, or at times inflicting a loss too, members of the society are becoming more and more vulnerable to act in a certain manner to live up to the society's expectations of them.

Social traps have always been a negative part of our society, but in recent times there has been a hike in it, especially among the youth. Social traps tend to focus more on short-term gains. One might think of it as somewhat twisted procrastination, where in spite of knowing how something can be saved from destruction, we let matters slide. Just how many times do we tend to overlook a leakage, ignoring it until one day the crack drifts apart and we end up in a far troubled state. We often choose to ignore a trivial task at home, labeling it as not our work and look for a fixer of a specific race, because this is how our minds have been tailored (majorly based on how others determined it). So when such a simple leakage issue could have been resolved, why do we not pay heed to it?

Such behavior can be linked to many things. From ignorance to human nature of stereotyping, to doing what most people expect of us. In this case, it is generalized that leakage will be fixed if it gets too serious, until then it can be left alone. We never seem to learn from our mistakes until it gets too late. We fail to realize that the concept behind social trap is to stop someone from doing something for their betterment, often to validate oneself. Also, these traps are based on stereotypical judgments and do not allow for breaking societal norms. Yes, we are still reluctant to change. This has been the case for African American families as well.

Social Traps Constraining African-American Families From Becoming High-Achievers

Social traps are one of the major hindrances for individuals. They are the roadblocks that prevent a person from continuing their journey or reaching higher platforms. Why? Because we let our minds be gullible to what others perceive of us. The human mind is the most gullible when an individual has undergone a trauma or grows up in a state of misfortune. More on this later. For now, I will expand on how these social traps are fairly common within the ghetto communities, and how they hinder the African-Americans from succeeding in their lives.

To grow with a lack of resources, to hear profanities as means of addressing someone, to suffer at the expanse of prejudice, and not be considered equal irrespective of holding a degree or requisite skills for a job, African-Americans are far vulnerable to social traps than they realize. They have grown up hearing how they either cannot perform a task or already have a predetermined course that they need to take, which poses a threat to their social standing even in their own community.

African-Americans living in the ghetto communities are reluctant to changes. Adopting one is already hard for them as an assertive denial is in store for them. They have been assured by the society they will not be granted the same status as someone with a contrasting skin tone. Living all their lives hearing of discrimination and witnessing it depletes the African American of any motivation or strength they have to achieve their dreams and reach a new milestone.

It is engraved in their minds due to the social traps that no matter what, they will never be at the same level as someone who is privileged. Those who do try to defy this norm are often a subject of mockery within their community as it clashes with the pre-determined image of a person from the hoods. We may not realize it, but our words are mightier than swords. Words that the society spoke to degrade the ghettos have seeped into the system of the *Blacks* living there for the worse.

"You can change your world by changing your words… remember, death and life are in the power of the tongue."

– Joel Osteen

Stereotyping African-Americans As A Threat Widens the Achievement Gap

As we understand how words have a deeper impact to make or break a person, we can see why the stereotypes associated with a person from the hood threaten the existence and future of the youth of the ghetto community. You can easily look for researches to support my words. You will come to see how stereotypes are venomous and real. They have the limitless power of crucifying a person's ability and motivation. It cripples the self-belief system of African-Americans as they continue to grow watching a life already created for them that is devoid of equal opportunities. From the females expected not to be great at math to the males being regarded as thugs, they feel obliged to live up to the societal expectations.

The stereotypes linked to ghetto communities are continuously widening the *achievement gap*, forming an impending threat to future generations. This achievement gap refers to the continuous failure of people belonging to a certain group. The achievement gap is not limited to just education, as students are already from low-income families, but goes as far as work and personal life too.

In spite of having all the skills and talents to be successful, since the words of the society have already poisoned the system of the African-Americans to live in impoverishment, the ghetto community has started to adhere to this. Each day, a person in the hood gives up on their dreams and picks up the life thrust their way. They lose their self-belief and instead pick up the belief of society, whereby they are not to surpass the odds of their life. When this happens, when a person starts telling themselves not to make any efforts because there is no point, the achievement gap in the hoods widens. I have seen so many people with ambition and immense talents, but I have watched most of them not working on themselves, because they think, *"What is the point, I will never have the same thing as someone with a lighter skin tone. Why should I waste my time working hard?"*

Performing Poorly Because You Are Expected To Be Weak

It is heartbreaking to hear someone give up on their dreams just because it is expected of us to be weak. We do not bother to prove the authoritative negativity wrong. Instead, we prove them right. This made me realize one thing, how we have made ourselves similar to a computer system. Our brain works in nearly the same fashion as a computer, but it is more enhanced on the emotional aspect. Hence, as you feed a computer with commands, you do the same with your brain. Why do you think you congratulate someone when they achieve something or express your remorse on their loss? Because your brain has been functioned this way. It is a command fed by the adults in your mind which you have adopted after observing them doing the same.

Likewise, being classified as troublemakers and watching the adults of the community struggle all their lives to make ends meet, the youngsters also accept that they are incapable of climbing out of stagnation. Let's explore a little more by category. Firstly, students know they belong to low-income families and will not be getting the same opportunity as a student from a privileged background. This leaves them to develop a mindset of focusing on finding ways to make a faster income than work on their future, as it will be in vain. They start to deem going to a college to be a far-fetched thought, hence they think why not work on earning money than to be working hard only for their efforts to go down the drain.

Secondly, young adults doubt their potential based on their skin color, henceforth they do not try for greater opportunities. In the end, they settle for less as they are glad to be employed. They fear to ask for an appraisal even when they know they are worthy because they also believe they are replaceable. This is engraved in the minds of the majority of African-Americans who continue to perform below average, just because everyone around them classifies them as *weak*.

Anxiety Is Closely Associated With Stereotyping, Affecting How A Person Acts

Continuously labeling people as weak affects them, no matter how much we want to deny this. This is human nature and cannot be changed, though it is controllable. A certain code of conduct is imposed on the ghetto community, where they feel burdened to act in a dissimilar way. If they act a little different, then they are considered *not quite black* by their own people.

It sounds unreal but this is the truth. There is a way that black people are supposed to act. Doing otherwise makes them laughable in the eyes of their own people. If a guy does not believe in violence, if he refuses to certain people, then he is considered to be weak. If a boy is not great at basketball and a female's vocal notes not high enough, there is nothing wrong with them. But their community starts to consider them *not black*. Even if their dressing is different than what a person from the hoods commonly wears, they are considered different.

It is already hard to cope with life when jobs are limited, finance is scarce, and dreams seem unreal. To add onto the burden, the ghetto community has to abide by the standards of their people, even if it begs to differ than what they want. Failing to do so starts to fill the black people with a sense of anxiety, which only piles up. This sort of anxiety is known as stereotype threat or stereotype anxiety. It mostly comes from racial discrimination where the victims feel obligated to act the same as their group, thus validating the stereotype developed in the first place. Most of the time when someone makes an effort to climb the social ladder that goes against the rules of being black and their own people look down at them, they feel the need to stop. Anxiety evolves from what is fed to our brain. If the ghetto community is continuously fed negativity, this will be all they know, and they will only know not to try and find comfort in that.

Be Your Own Person, Unconfined To The Stereotype And Expectations Dictated To You

Knowing how society plays a part in cutting the roots of someone else's growth, ask yourself, why are you giving them this much power over you? Should these people who do not contribute to your growth but are living a life of ease themselves matter to you? No. Stereotypes should be broken. It is always easier said than done, but if your mind can accept negativity, then it can surely accept positivity. You need to realize that you are unable to do things in life only until you allow yourself to do those things. Remember, no one else can stunt your growth but yourself.

Achievement gaps can be overcome by establishing an attitude of *no excuses*. Yes, ghetto communities have found safety in denial than wanting to break out of their comfort zone. Taking risks seems scary, but if you don't take them, you will never know. Ask yourself, do you want to be in a better place? If the answer is yes, then you can change it simply by telling yourself that you can do it.

It will not happen in a day or two but will take time. After all, the damage incurred is worth many years, but you can alter your path. You do not have to victimize yourself. Life is unfair, it will never treat anyone better. This should not mean we are entitled to weakness or show strength through an aggressive state. Stereotypic traits associated with a black person, especially spread through the wrongful usage of the power of social media, do not define you. What other people inside and outside your community expect of you does not define you either. They cannot *dictate* you who you are.

You are your own person. I am too. I was in your shoes, but I chose to believe that I can go further, I can climb the highest peak of the mountain. So, I started to tell my brain that I can do the same task that another person is doing until my brain believed that and changed my course. I managed to grow, which was what made me emphasize the saying – *work now, ball later.*

Start working on yourself, even if your effort is worth half a drop of water. Rivers were not formed overnights. It took each drop to form something enormous. You can do the same. Just do not confine yourself to the standards of society and start teaching yourself self-belief.

Chapter 5

Cost of Opportunist

*"Stay away from lazy parasites, who perch on you just to satisfy
their needs, they do not come to alleviate your
burdens, hence, their mission is to distract, detract and extract, and
make you live in abject poverty."*

— *Michael Bassey Johnson*

We are living in times where more people are willing to take up the opportunity present to them at all costs, even when they don't deserve it. I guess this is why people prefer bootlicking tactics and learning how to fake their talent to get the position over another person who deserves it rightfully. Such a deed is often done by the unexpected most person whom we trust blindly.

Our present is dark and the future is bleak. While half of the world is struggling to rebuild self-belief within themselves and the people around them because they know the predicament of self-doubts and how vexing it can be, there are a few who make the most by seizing an opportunity from someone else. You might have found yourself sharing an opportunity with someone, only to find out later that the same person has made the most of it. Just by sharing information about a promising job opportunity, you often find that person at that position. Why? Because they took the opportunity before you could. If you find yourself in a similar position, then let's try to put an end to it.

The Cost Of Opportunist

It is not a bad thing to have an opportunistic mindset, but if it comes at the cost of taking away from someone, especially knowing how that person has worked hard, it is bad. There is no other way to put it. We need to work on our own opportunities and not be a parasite who leeches on the opportunity of another person.

We do not know of the struggles a person goes through. Such an opportunist who waits to strive at the opportunity of another is, as told above, often within our closest circle. These people are around only in search of an achievement they can label as theirs. This is not the only type of opportunist we find ourselves surrounded by. Some of them may be our existing friends or partners, who are around for a personal gain. Be it a relationship or work, an opportunist puts on a mask of being a well-wisher. As soon as they find something that benefits them, they avail it, be it any cost, even at the cost of betraying their business partner and friends. Often in ghetto communities where resources are limited, our closest friends can be our foe.

African-Americans do not usually get greater opportunities at work, and so when one individual works hard, they share the news with their friends in excitement. Soon, one of the friends is discovered to be taking up that position. Such friends are the rotten apple hiding in a bunch of fresher ones, leaving a person hurt.

Importance Of Friends – Good & Bad

Just because we are betrayed by a friend does not mean we need to cut off entirely from people. No, there are good and bad people. In life, we encounter both and it is crucial to experience betrayal too. Because if you are never to experience this, you will never realize the importance of a good friend. There are all sorts of people around us as we are not clones of one another. Different people in life make us realize the importance of the good ones and make us be aware of the bad ones.

Friends are the people who believe in us. On days when we find ourselves drenched in a storm, a good friend will come for our aid. Friends tend to provide support, in any way they can. We need to learn not to rely on anyone. In life, we will come across various situations where what we need the most is another soul. On days when one cannot meet their eye in the mirror, they will need someone else to show them their beauty.

We have discussed the importance of words in the previous chapter. Words of encouragement do miracles. But where do these words come from? They come from family and friends. These people are our supporters. They become our light in the darkness and our reason to smile when we are going through a slump in life. At the same time, we are prone to getting backstabbed, so how can we prevent it?

Identifying Fake Friends

If you have a basket full of apples, in which there is a rotten one, will you throw the entire basket out? No. Similarly, just because you have one bad friend does not mean you should go cutting your ties with other friends who truly care for you. There are friends with whom when we spend time, we feel lighter. Then there are people whom we dread meeting, for they always tend to be needy of favors. In spite of doing well, they are too cynical, too judgmental, and seem to take pleasure in roasting jokes that are based on your insecurities.

No friend should ever exploit your insecurity, because if they do, then this is the very first sign of a fake friend. Friendship is based on care without self-motive. So, if a friend of yours is in touch with you only to ask for something but disappears when you are in need of something, it means you're in the company of a fake friend. You may find yourself always being there for such friends, even in situations where you will have to bail them out for improper conduct, but if you ever need to vent to them, you will find them ditching you.

Ask yourself this: are friends to abandon another in distress? You should not be doing a favor to your friend by helping them out or expecting them to return that favor someday. But friends are supposed to be there for one another. Often a friend might not be there as they can be going through a situation of their own. But friends who only surface when they are in need and refuse to be there for you when you are in need, are taking advantage of you.

Really, we are surrounded by people who are in our life just to invalidate us more than people who actually stop us from making a wrongful decision that can harm us. But we can miss out on the many signs of such people. Through this section, you will be able to at least figure out if you have any fake friends in your social circle or not.

Friends who tend to laugh at your plans than telling you to try aren't entirely good for your mental health too. If you ever find yourself sharing an idea about career and your friend counteracts by stating how you're being foolish, you will find yourself discouraged and will leave things instead of working and trying. In a similar situation, if your friend encourages you to try something after highlighting the risks and motivates you to take a risk because you won't ever know the outcome until you go for it, then that particular friend is someone you should value and appreciate.

Fake friends are like a drain plug who can drain away positivity from you. Similarly, good friends fill you with motivation and self-belief, filling your wings with air so that they can watch you soar high.

Learning How To Say No

Like I have stated above, friendship should not come with a cost. If you do something for your friends, it should be out of love and care. If you find your friend in need of help and can offer them help, then do so. Do not expect anything in return, but do not let anyone take undue advantage of your friendship as well where it will soon start coming at the cost of losing something you worked hard for.

Learning how to identify the snake living under your sleeve allows you to stop them from taking advantage of you. If someone is truly a friend, they will understand your reasons and respect them. When someone calls you out for refusing to help them without understanding your reason, it is best to maintain a safer distance. You do not always have to be there for a person who is prone to making decisions that are wrong and then counts on you to come to their rescue.

Be cautious of who you share your happiness with because envy and anger are sins that can corrupt anyone. If a friendship is stressing you out due to people being unjust and unreasonable, it is absolutely acceptable to distance yourself. If a friend is coming up to you when they have gotten themselves into trouble, and helping them may endanger your rapport, know it is perfect to say *no* to them.

Getting Rid Of Snakes Is Better

In life, you come across many types of friendships. Some as old as a decade, while some as new as yesterday. You come to realize that you have a deeper connection with friends you have known for the shortest of time as compared to those you have known since a young age. You may share the same interests with colleagues and better collaboration with just an associate. So if time does not determine the kind of friendship you establish with people, then what does?

It is human nature to befriend someone with mutual interest. However, sometimes people don't need mutual interests to be friends with someone. It seems there is another factor involved in being friends with someone – an unknown reason. You do not need to have a good reason why you're friends with that someone. With these friends of yours, you may find yourself questioning, *"Why am I friends with them?"* This is the sort of friendship you need to steer clear of in the ghetto communities, for such friendships come with a cost.

Certain friends of yours make you question them due to their attributes and behavior. These friends are toxic. They are the ones constantly complaining to you in the hopes of you doing them a favor. They exploit something you would have told them in secrecy. They take advantage of an opportunity you worked hard for. What do you do in such a friendship then?

When it comes to friendship, situations are delicate and tricky. Your words can hurt your friends. However, this should not compel you to remain friends with people who are toxic to your health. Just like how we end toxic relationships, we need to put an end to being in the company of those who pose any form of threat to us in the ghetto communities, without being disrespectful or rude.

A simple *no* suffices when they ask you for something. Maintaining distance from such *so-called* friends can help you achieve your goals and get you out of the hoods. Be mindful of the reason you give to them. Remember, you do not need to divulge all your information. Only by avoiding such people, you will see a positive effect on your life. That shall be the day you will realize it is better to get rid of snakes!

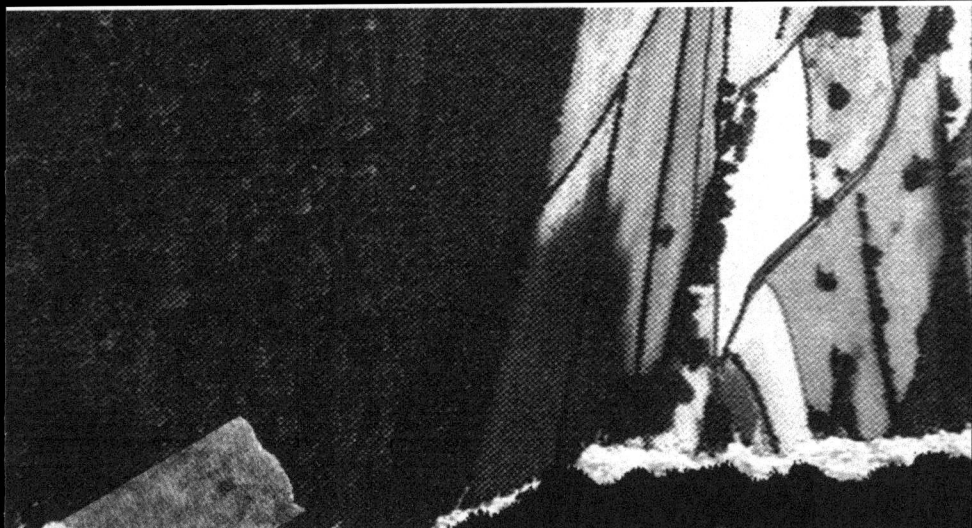

Chapter 6

Passing Power

"In vain have you acquired knowledge if you have not imparted it to others."

- Deuteronomy Rabbah

Knowledge Is Power

In life, we have come this far and all of it is owed to the evolution of things. A tedious process of remodeling the olden methodologies and code of conduct in life. From using animals for transportation to making vehicles, everything around us has evolved. It wouldn't be wrong if we say that every change achieved so far was made possible by acquiring knowledge.

Knowledge is just as crucial to existence as clean air and water. Knowledge fuels our mind to work to its full capacity. Without knowledge, we would never have come this far to having cars and skyscrapers. We would still have been stuck living in caves like cavemen.

Knowledge is the key that unlocks endless portals of life. It pushes every individual to go beyond their standing point in life. It allows for a person to constantly achieve greater heights. At the same time, it is something that is constantly gained. We never stop gaining knowledge and we should never either, because it is the ultimate treasure in life that comes free and is infinite. Remember, knowledge unchains a person's stagnated state.

If we stop our mind from gaining more knowledge, it is the same as depriving ourselves of oxygen, without which our system turns stale. Without knowledge, a person can never progress in life. This may sound like a rather strong and bias statement, but it is prudent. We witness this daily in our life when we compare people.

Ignorance Within The African-American Community

We understand how important knowledge is when it comes to working, be it at home or at the workplace. It triggers a chain of series for you to move forward from your current state. One step leads to another. As you continue with this chain, you end up reaching your destination.

But what happens when you don't have this knowledge? What happens when you remain ignorant? You are unable to reach your destination. You remain standing at one point. Such is the case for African-Americans, living in the hoods deprived of knowledge. Some of the ghetto communities are still held back from competing with the ordinary lives of many only because they do not know how to do so.

I have talked about never saying no to knowledge as we are continuously gaining it, but how do we actually gain such an unparalleled thing? You see, knowledge comes with exposure. The more you are exposed to your current world, the more you are aware of what is happening and how. From there, you either adopt the same ideology or are able to enhance your own, based on the current standing of the world. You are able to think for yourself when you are exposed to varying perspectives buzzing around you.

But such exposure comes to a person stepping out of their zone and into a new one. This is a luxury. I say this because not everyone is able to afford exposure that helps you gain knowledge.

The cost of gaining knowledge is often not available to African-American households on the basis of either racial discrimination or poverty and in some cases both. Simply put, the ghetto communities continue to remain ignorant of knowledge at large because they are unable to afford it.

Challenges That the African-American Youth Faces

Without knowledge, the African-American youth is unaware of the talent they possess, because of which they fail to utilize and enhance their existing skills. Even if the African-American youth, living in the hoods, realizes the need to change their life, they are unable to do so. Why? Because their parents are ignorant of knowledge. Access to information is limited for the youth. Consequently, they fall downhill as all they have ever observed is hardships, dependency, racial discrimination, abuse, and whatnot.

The society has stigmatized the ghetto youth to be the exact same as their elders. When this constant nagging is preached to them and shown, they grow accustomed to it. They choose to stay in the comfort zone because if they try to step out of it, they are mocked. The reason behind it is the lack of literacy and recognition of good and bad. Words have the power to make or break a person. So if the youth in the hoods hears negative things about them, how can they ever make a positive impact on the world?

Importance Of Knowledge In The Hoods

Knowledge is what empowers a person to move forward. How else can you work something out when you do not have any clue about it. One cannot even light the stove if they do not have the knowledge about doing so.

See, even the simplest of things in life can be out of reach for most people, and it is usually the poverty-stricken who suffer. Why? Because they do not have the right exposure to knowledge and advancement in life. The poverty-stricken people are those who only know the archaic way to life. They are unaware of how far we have progressed.

Similarly, due to the lack of proper education in the hoods, the youth only perceives life as good or bad. Life is black or white for them as that's all they have been taught. But if they are taught about the gray areas in life, it will broaden their perspective. It will remove the blindfold from their eyes and help them see there is more to life, which they can achieve too.

Right now, the youth is paralyzed in the sense that the society has somewhat decided a set of life for them, where they just do what their elders have been doing. However, if the youth in the hoods is taught how they can think for themselves, how they can make their decisions, they will certainly make the most of their life. Right now, so many young people yearn for a better life, but due to their underprivileged state, they can only yearn for it or acquire it through illicit means, as crime is expected of them due to their heritage.

Passing Power To The Youth

"If you have the knowledge, let others light their candles in it."

- Margaret Fuller

Without knowledge, a child cannot walk. This is why the adults teach the child the basic skills, of communication and walking, in life. No one is born with the knowledge, you see. No one knows how to stand, eat, or speak as they are born, but with time as the child grows, their families teach them all of that. From etiquette to education, the knowledge the adults gain from their elders, they continue to pass it on. Why? Because if they won't, the child would remain crippled.

In life, as you grow, you gain wisdom and knowledge that helps you progress in life. If you refrain from gaining the knowledge, your pool of awareness and recognition will remain null, much like the youth in the ghetto community. They do not have the rightful access to exposure and learning, leading them to remain unenlightened. Due to lack of finance, the African American youth is quick to follow the footsteps of their adults, leaving them to be stuck in a loop of low progress. Their life remains dark as they have no means to bring light.

The youth is our future. If they have no one to teach them, to bring them out of their standstill position in life, they will never know what exploring means. Let's look at it this way. If an adult refuse to teach a child how to stand, they will never be able to walk. Imagine a child who doesn't know how to stand, in a literal sense. Your mind must be bursting with *"Oh my goodness, how will the child go to school or work?"*

Similarly, if you do not teach the African-American youth how to stand up and walk figuratively, how can you expect them to progress despite having the ability. You hold the torch in your hand, but you refuse to share the light with them. If you fail to share your wisdom, it is given that the African-American youth will continue to walk in the dark. You have the power to share your knowledge with them and empower them to reach greater heights of success.

This is what motivated me to write this book in the first place. I managed to get out of the dark because apart from self-belief and wanting to improve my life, I searched for wisdom from others who shared their strengths and struggles with me. So, if that can change my life, imagine how many lives we can touch by sharing the power of knowledge. Reach the youth living in the hoods, give them a chance, and you will see the difference that you will be making by sharing something as priceless as knowledge.

RIALTO, CA

Chapter 7

Focus on What You Can Control

Relationship, Resources, and Dedication

"It is during our darkest moments that we must focus to see the light."

– Aristotle

Importance Of Taking Control

In life, nothing comes with a guarantee. Situations arise, accidents happen, and it is always easier said than done when someone tries to console us. We find the words of encouragement during our darkest moment to be fabricated hope. We start to lose our mind bit by bit until we turn blind to our surroundings.

Stop and take a deep breath. In life, no one of us has the best of it. A person might have wealth, but they might not have contentment, peace, love, happiness, or even friendship. We all are blessed in one way or another. Only when we are struck by a predicament, we start to lose control. What little we have goes down the drain. As the light threatens to go out, the thought of being surrounded by darkness is devastating.

At the same time, none of us can fit the shoes of another. Every one of us has to walk the path of life. Even if our destination is the same, the journey is quite unlike. Our lives are different. At times it is colored with smiles and pleasant times. At other times we feel like a raining cloud is placed right above our heads. Some of us do deal with the worst of times and fail to find our way out, leaving us to lose control of the navigation of our lives.

So, what happens when you lose control, instead of regaining it? You lose your sense of direction and life starts to feel overwhelming. You panic, you get frightened, and you worry endlessly. While it is human instinct to react in such a manner, none of this helps in the long run. In the long run, what helps to get back on track is the need for you to pick yourself back up and continue walking even when you have hurt your feet. Because if you stop, if you cave into a setback, you will never be able to control your life.

However, I understand there are limitations to this. During some of our harshest moments, we end up being far more hurt and confused by the happenings of life that we need to rely on someone else to help us out. How? Let's find out.

Expanding Your Pool For Networking Outside The Hoods

When we are going through troubled times, we find it best to lock up our feelings instead of relying on someone else for support. It's easier not to confide in someone else for reasons like fear of being exploited or made fun of. What we fail to see is that by cutting ties and connections, we are in a way contributing to losing control of our life.

When we meet with people and share something with them, be it our emotions, our current circumstance, or our passion, it opens up doors we didn't know were there. Life within the hoods is already hard, with unemployment always on the rise within the ghetto communities. Sometimes, people end up losing their jobs, and the lot that is lucky enough to be employed fails to make ends meet of the families. In such an environment, very little African-Americans can survive if they wish to start a business venture of their own.

The main reason behind this is that many people from the hoods are comfortable only in their own circle. Within their circle, they continue to struggle as the aspiring entrepreneurs find it hard to carry on with their ventures. When we refuse to step outside the hoods, we are cutting down on more than just building a better relationship with the world around us. We are crippling our confidence by allowing self-doubts to prevail. This is the first step toward failure. If you want to step out of the hoods and make a life for yourself, how can you do so if you lack the basic confidence of striking a conversation?

Likewise, we already know it is hard to find opportunities within the ghetto communities. The existing businesses are already suffering, then how can you expect anyone rendering you even hope when you don't put in the efforts to build a relationship. We fail to realize that when we interact with another person, it boosts our confidence and builds our human skills, which is what gets half the job done. Also, interacting with others brings us a step closer to finding the right mentors, suppliers, ideas, and whatnot.

The point is that opportunities to interact with resourceful people might not be present within the ghetto communities, and the world outside is not half as bad as the African-Americans think it is. It would take stepping out of the hoods to realize that.

Accumulating Resources From Within The African-American Communities And Outside

When it comes to facing hardships and we try to grasp the idea of regaining control of our life, ideas brim in our head. I can remember vividly when I was trying to figure out a business idea for myself. It was hard and terrifying. At the same time, to be able to make a living for myself, as well as being my own boss, just fueled the idea of controlling what I could do.

However, as I was busy daydreaming, I realized one basic thing that I lacked resources. That was the moment I felt my heart stop. I had no resources and I was busy planning an entire business in my head. Now, I had two options. Either I give up on my idea and return to struggling in the hoods or I believe in myself and work toward fixing the obstacle of lacking resources.

My fear led me to be scared and unconvincing everywhere I went in the hopes of searching for investors and suppliers. My idea turned weak as I was unable to stand in front of all these different people. A few of them were familiar faces of the African-Americans I used to know. They refused to help me out as they were unable to believe in my vision. Now when I look back, I realize they were not wrong to have done so. Because how could they believe in my vision when I wasn't myself?

I will expound on this in the next segment, but this was what led me to step out. I wanted to achieve all that I was visualizing in my head, forcing me to step out and interact with people from even outside the hoods. Hence, I met so many people, mostly those who believed in me and helped me build *Over the World*. You see, not always we can find resources within the African-American communities. There are times in life when we need to step out of our comfort zone in the hopes of accumulating resources that benefit us and help us in life.

Dedication Is The Key To Moving Forward

All of that stated above sounds attainable, right? Just a little bit of effort for you to take a step out of the hoods to find the right way. But when the time comes to taking such a step actually, quite a fraction of the youth from the African-American communities seems to falter. Suddenly, doubts prevail and most of us are left to doubt our own worth. Thus, it becomes easy to shut down on the thought of achieving something than working toward it.

Furthermore, belonging to the hoods comes with the skeptic and snide remarks of the people around us. For an odd reason, others seek happiness by belittling another. You know, words are mightier than a sword. The words of discouragement like *"Oh why bother? You are wasting your time," "You aren't good enough,"* and *"You are black, how you think you can succeed?"* actually have the power to kill someone's drive to excel in their future.

You can have control over what you want, you can have a detailed plan set up, you can have the rightful connections and sources, but at the end of the day, if your dedication deters, you will fail to move forward. Yes, all of the above-mentioned attributes toward you fulfilling your dream will turn into a daydream if one day you find yourself losing your dedication. Dedication is the same as fuel. It drives you to strive and achieve your goals. The society African-Americans live in makes it easy for a person to give up than to succeed. Thus, to bring a change, you need to take measures in your hands. Dedication is the key that will unlock the door to your future. Once you start thinking of hard work as useless for whatever reason, you will remain stagnant in life.

Dedication Goes Hand In Hand With Resources If You Want To Go Further In Life

If you are not dedicated to something, then it's definitely not worth it. So, first figure out what is it that you truly want to achieve. Life is getting harder day by day. With the rising cost of living, it is easier to fall in the easy ways of making an income. Due to the stigma this society has placed on the African-Americans, it doesn't come to me as a surprise why the African-American youth falls into the pattern they have seen all their life.

You need to understand and make yourself see this. By doing so, you choose to push your will and motivation to do better in life.

Right now, if an idea has struck you, do not abandon it. Instead, care for it and nurture it. You can do so by interacting with more people, building new relationships, and talking to more and more people. Talk about your idea and what you wish to do with that. Build a cycle of hope for yourself where you try daily, even if you fail.

Define your goal and work on it. Break down things, align all the resources you have gathered. You will soon see that these steps will lead you to create a puzzle of your dreams. Then, once the puzzle pieces lie before you, you might find yourself losing all hope and motivation to continue with it. But you need to see this is the moment things get real. This is the point that signifies you are closer to achieving your dreams than ever. Because if you are still far away, your subconsciousness will have to remain relaxed. If your subconsciousness is making you fret and lose hope, it means you're getting closer to achieving your dream. Just don't give up hope.

Once you feel the fear settling down within you, it proves that you actually want to achieve this particular dream. This is the time for you to sit down and tell yourself that you have to commit. Because real is to be scary, and if it is real, it is worth it. I hope you realize that without dedication and commitment, all of your efforts and planning are a waste. So if you wish to walk through the door to your bright future, you have to choose to keep the key of dedication with you. If not, you will only end up with a lifetime of *what if.*

Chapter 8

The Hand We Are Dealt

"You may not control all the events that happen to you, but you can decide not to be reduced by them."

- Maya Angelou

Life does not always deal with us in the same way. Some of us go through experiences that are enough to scar us for life. Still, there is a person we all know of whose story is no secret from the world. We find her the most humble and full of life, with a smile brighter than the stars. Yes, I am talking about Oprah Winfrey.

From being born out of wedlock to a teenage mother, having to live with her grandmother due to poverty and being raped, Oprah endured what was a horror story of a few African-American neighborhoods. She had enough reasons to fall into the pattern of life she saw. After all, she was deprived of opportunities. The roof above her head was shared, her family had little on its table, and there was no proper guidance. She had enough reasons to succumb to the vicious pattern of the ghetto community like a few youths tended to do, of possibly getting marriage at a young age and not believing in education. Only, she did not.

In spite of the ill-fate and sufferings, Oprah held her head high and continued to walk until the opportunity came before her.

She must not have the slightest of a clue of what tomorrow was to bring, yet she took the chance and continued to hope for a better tomorrow. With the same belief, she went to live with her father and made the most of the chance she was given. The rest is history as we all know. From wearing overalls made from potato sacks to high-end designers, she is the epitome of wonder and miracles.

Do Not Use The Hood Life As An Excuse

The reason I have used Oprah Winfrey's story is to inspire every person reading this. Her childhood was berserk. She had no escape or anyone to stand up for her and demand justice. Likewise, there are so many more names that I can take that had a fate similar to hers until they changed it. So many people have made a name for themselves, despite their traumatic childhood experiences.

When a person goes through a catastrophe, they are sure to incur wounds. But if given time, the wounds heal, leaving behind scars. Those scars serve as a constant reminder of what the individual had to go through. While some hide it, others embrace it. Oprah could have hidden her past, but she did not. This is another thing I highlighted in the previous chapters. Having gone through something bad in your past does not need to overshadow your future. You do not have to be embarrassed by all that you endured. Also, you do not have to be embarrassed about being an African American who does not hail from a privileged background. As long as you are willing to change, trust me, you can be the pinnacle of strength.

Moving on, if you are someone whose life was difficult in the hoods but are now living your dream, do take some time out and visit your old ghetto community. Your story depicts an endless struggle that managed to find some solace in this life. You might not realize it, but you will be the candle whose mere words will light up the lives of endless youth. Life in the hoods has never been easy since the beginning of time. Endless forms of discrimination and abuse exist even today. From teenage mothers struggling to keep a roof above their heads to overconsumption of intoxication. The younglings do not frequently get a chance to hear of hope and positivity. If you can offer that to someone, then why hold back your words? Do visit any African-American community near you and share your story with them. Who knows, you might inspire a soul or two for the better?

Within the African-American communities, a few families are intact, but they can barely pay the bills and have a meal on their table. There are families where young boys have fallen into selling narcotics and illicit items and girls have turned into thugs in the hopes of escaping the abuse that echoes in their houses. There are families with abusive parents who show their children to rely on intoxication as a means to escape the pain. There are families that sleep on an empty stomach and are denied jobs just because of their dark skin color. After witnessing all this, we still fail to understand why the hoods are exposed to such treatments and bias living standards.

None of this means you should deprive yourself of keeping hope alive in your heart. What do you think keeps a person afloat? From my understanding, there are two things. The first is belief and the second is not playing the blame game. It is very easy to understand. When you choose to believe, you are telling yourself that there is hope. With this thought, you feel wanting to go beyond. Thus, if you ever dream of moving out of the hoods, then you need to tell yourself to continue believing. If someone else can do it, if I can do it, then so can you. Just believe.

Play The Hand You Are Dealt With

Life comes with endless trials that we have to overcome. There are nights when so many people within the ghetto communities go to sleep, not wanting to wake up the next day. Growing up in a harsh environment where tomorrow comes with uncertainty, where wasting time and blaming our situation is normalized, we fail to understand the actual loss that we are incurring. There's no denying the fact that life is especially hard for a child who has only ever witnessed trauma. But all of this can be changed and you yourself have that power.

These words may sound like a fabricated hope to you, although they are not. You do have the power to alter the course of your life, however, you can only do so by accepting it. Now we all are aware of how denial and acceptance work. When you choose to deny the truth, you are trying to block out your predicaments and it is absolutely understandable. Nobody wants to be reminded of all they have endured. The struggles and hardships. But, when we choose to ignore them, we are ending our chance to resolve those very issues.

When you choose *to accept*, it means you are willing to look at your troubled time. By doing so, you are willing to accept all that happens, whether good or bad. When you look into all you have gone through, somewhere among the reflection you will find a solution. When you are in pain, your mind naturally blocks out anything and everything that can hurt you. Choosing to deal with your pain allows your brain to be open to everything and each possibility starts to surface before you.

Let's go back to Oprah Winfrey's story. She never once ran away from all that she went through but used her sufferings to make her stronger. When she accepted it all, she took power to go through any storm in life despite never deserving either of it. She chose to believe in the person she was rather than letting her *hood life* dictate her future. She wanted a future for herself and achieved a future from her humble background. She dealt with the hand that was first trying to cripple her and made peace with it.

How did Oprah do so? It is not by playing the blame game. Instead of victimizing herself, she saw herself as a survivor. If she came out of all the pain alive, it signified just how strong she was. She accepted everything, leading her to walk out of her life.

We are quick to victimize ourselves. While it is fine for the moment, it soon builds our habit of feeling bad for ourselves constantly. This makes us lose focus and we forget to resolve the issue. We get too comfortable knowing how we were done wrong in life than to change that around. We are left with nothing then. But, if we make peace and accept our life in the hoods, we will be at ease enough to look for options and work out. All of the cards that we are dealt with in the world, we do not need to blame it on them, but give time to learn how to use them.

Strive For Your Goals Irrespective Of Your Current Standstill Position

No matter what happens, never give up. Remember, the moment you choose to feel sorry for yourself is the very moment that you lose it all. Then you can continue to blame the hood life you want. But if there is even a trivial part within you that wants a way out, you need to tell your mind to stop. Stop, take a deep breath, and exhale, then continue to walk. If you are breathing now, you are meant to go further in life. So, who are you to turn your thoughts cynic and deny your abilities?

Sometimes, it is our own fault that we fail to progress. We are holding on to our existing situation too tightly. We need to understand that there comes a time when we have to let go of our past. Our past does not define our future. We are not the same person we were yesterday. Every day you grow and every day is different. If this is the norm of life, then why do we not adopt this habit? Try once, twice, and then trice. Build a drift of trying. Even when you fail, trying won't hurt you. You won't lose anything from trying endlessly except for an opportunity someday. Remember, the only thing that hurts you is by constantly thinking about your past.

You need to start building goals for yourself and continue dreaming. This way, every time life tries to push you down, your heart will remind you to continue hanging on. Draw up a chart with your goal. Every day write your progress and put it up somewhere

where you can see it for the entire day. It will serve as the visual of what you want. When you see something positive, when you see your progress, you will find yourself learning how to grow. From there your battle to achieve your goals will become easier than yesterday.

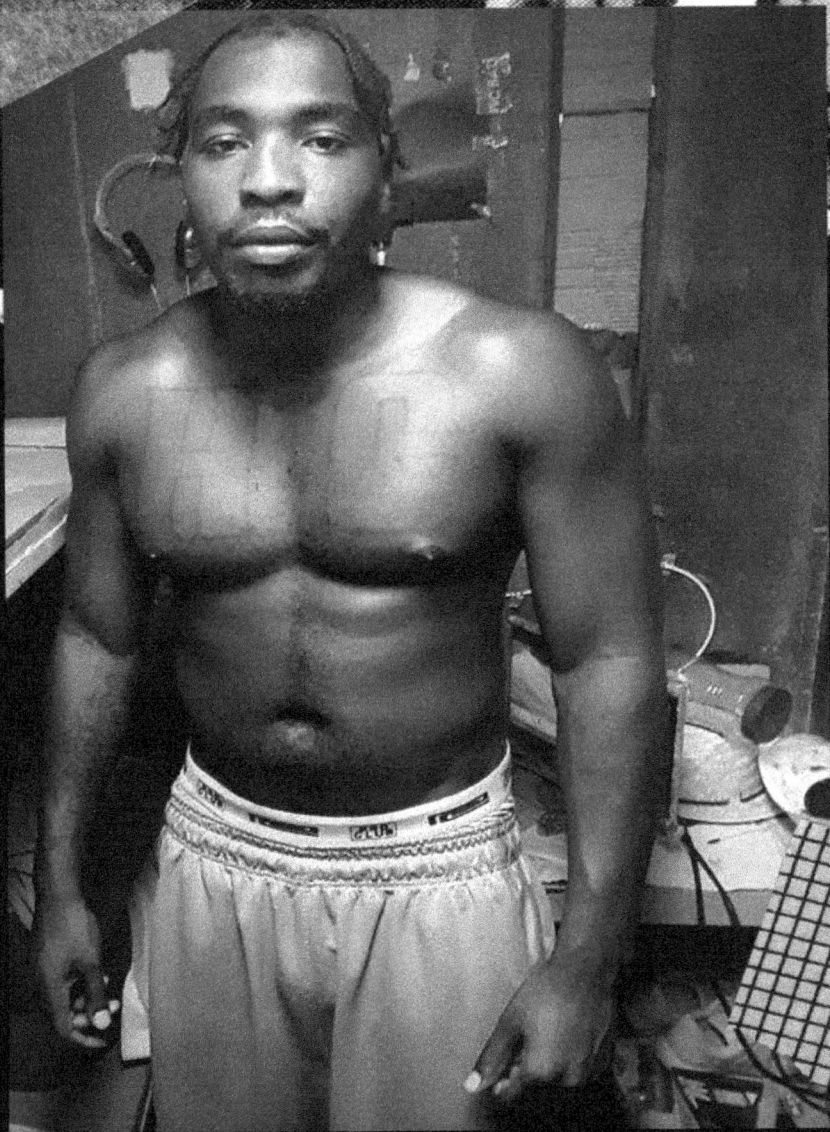

Chapter 9

Purpose of Transition

Open Doors for the Ones Coming Behind You

"No one is useless in this world who lightens the burdens of another."

— *Charles Dickens*

You Can Extend Your Services To Those In Need

Life is getting harder day by day. Resources are diminishing, opportunities are limited, and growth is stunted. In times when people are still getting jobs on the basis of sources rather than their set of skills, the African-Americans continue to face a threat at large. Yes, the education system within the hoods is trying to improve itself in the hopes of providing their future generations with a better tomorrow. The youth continues to face the underlying threat of giving up even before their life begins.

As I stumbled upon this reality, I tried to understand what makes the younger ones fall out? What makes them not want to excel in their education? I realized that their elders who are jobless, despite being educated, make them not want to invest their time in studying. The same goes for most people in the hoods. Children around us are naïve. As they grow, their young minds are molded. But due to growing up in the hoods, their minds are conditioned to a turbulent life. As a result, they end up doing what they feel the most comfortable at.

However, all of this can be overturned. As I understood that society holds power to make an impact on everyone's mind and decision-making ability, what if we use this power positively? So, instead of showcasing the negative, what if those of us, who managed to come out of the ghetto communities and make a living for ourselves, return to show what we achieved. All we have to do is extend our help to those in need and we can set a chained series of positive events until a change is made.

Pave A Path Out Of The Hoods For Everyone

Belonging to a ghetto community myself, I am well aware of how hard it is to build a living for yourself when you are already struggling to put a piece of bread in your stomach. Our lives can serve as a positive example and leave an impact on all the minds within the hoods that they do not have to comply with what their seniors did. They have a choice as we had, and we availed. If people like you and me, who are now making a good living of our own, return to extend our service of help, we can open a gateway of opportunities for the rest.

Looking back at my life, I remember there were times when I wished I could rely on someone. I wished I had a shoulder to cry on without the fear of my situation being exploited. But it was hard to find someone I could even share my problems with. I did not want to come off as needy. I just wanted someone to tell me that everything would be alright. Such a simple thing I found was the hardest to source in the hoods.

For an odd reason, it was fairly common that crying about your problems resulted in the people around you sharing their own issues. In those moments, I found encouragement the most. These were the people who somehow paved a path for me. The path that was less traveled in the hoods. Looking at those people, I could see they were the ones in the same living condition as me, but they were not afraid of making their own path. Even when people laughed at them for being whimsical, they walked out in search of a better life. When I followed their footsteps, I left that path behind me instead of closing it. Now, I wish to let other's walk on it too. I paved a path. Now I want that to serve as a bridge for everyone else. Maybe, like how I was inspired by others, more people can lead those in need and put them back on their feet with their words of encouragement.

A Majestic Tree Never Refuses To Shadow Those In Need

"A tree is known by its fruit; a man by his deeds. A good deed is never lost; he who sows courtesy reaps friendship, and he who plants kindness gathers love."

- Saint Basil

Have you ever observed a tree closely? How strong its bark is? You can tell so much of a tree by just looking at its bark. The sturdier it is, the deeper its roots are. Its crown is widespread, and the tree wears it with pride, letting all the branches spread out into twigs that hold the leaves in place. But the tree was not always this majestic. In the beginning, its growth must have been swift for it to form, but then must have come the point of transition where the tree must have craved something more until it nurtured itself and grew with time. Due to its strong roots, a tree can give life to endless leaves that form its crown. That very crown spreads out the shelter that is free for all living beings who seek it.

Similarly, if you find yourself having grown out of your hardship and you have achieved your goals, you will end up feeling a void within you. That is the moment in life when you want to do something more. So why not be a majestic tree for someone else? If you want your roots to strengthen over time, why not reach those in distress and help them? You have that power, just like a majestic tree. Does the tree ever refuse shelter to others? No. So why should you?

As a person who managed to stand on his two feet, I realized it is my responsibility now to teach others the walk of life. I know I have the power to let my shade reach out and provide relief to the scorching life of another. As I did so, I found myself happier than ever, even happier than when I had created something of my own. As a person hailing from the African-American community, I deem it my responsibility, as it is yours, to help those around you seeking shelter. Do not cower from help, because by helping others, you will find yourself far more accomplished than anything.

Keep The Door Open For Others Behind You

If you know what struggle is like, why would you want someone else to go through that? It takes time, sweat, blood, and tears to open a door that serves as a gateway to your great. There would have been a time in your life when you wished to rely on another for support. Taking that exact moment, you would have understood it is not necessary for help to come in the form of finance. Words of encouragement, kindness, mentorship, and any other form of guidance and consolation have been priceless.

Usually, this is the main reason why people mostly hesitate when it comes to helping others. They feel there is a certain underlying code, whereby if you are helping someone, you might need to help them financially as well. But this is not true. Help can come in the simplest form of even a smile that reaches your heart. You can help someone by just showing them how strong they are through your words. At times, a hug can suffice in stopping someone from ruining their life.

Help does not need to come in an exorbitant form. You can share your life with someone, and it can bring light to their life. You can just stand next to a person and help can come in the form of simply being around. The truth is help is anything that exits from one heart to enter another with the objective of healing. So, instead of closing the door that you opened, allow others to walk through it. Instead of shutting a door on someone, by letting them walk through it will bring you wealth that is priceless.

In life, you will come to see that it is far easier to acquire materialistic wealth, but when it comes to gaining inner peace, no amount of money can buy you that. Your own happiness will come easy when you realize you are the reason behind someone's smile and behind transforming someone's life for the good. When someone needs you just to provide a listening ear and you lend yours to them, it might help that person overcome an obstacle in life. When that happens, you will feel happier than them. Let kindness be the ultimate wealth of yours and share your strength with your own community and with your home.

OVER THE WORLD

LOS ANGELES

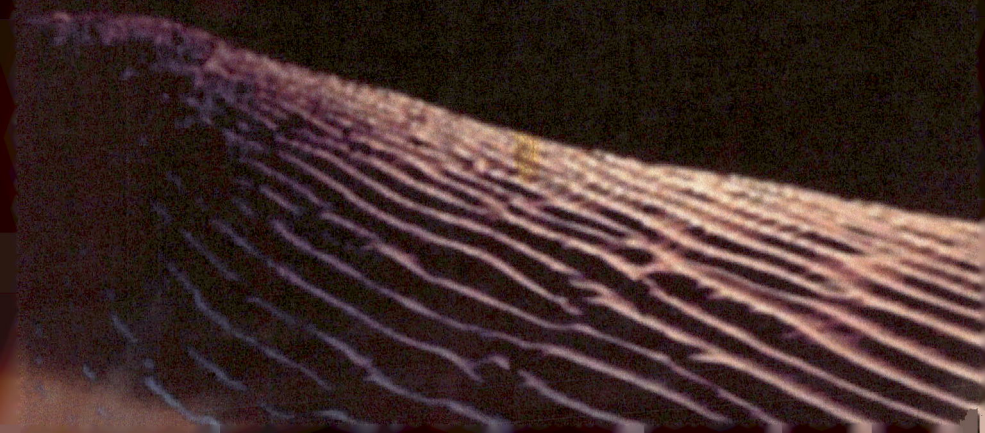

Chapter 10

The Beginning

No Matter How Many Times You Level Up, It Is the Beginning.

This book has been a summary of my life's journey up until now. All that inspired me in life, I have shared each of that wisdom with you. For every one of us on this earth, life is a journey with endless ups and downs. A rollercoaster as we often label it. We know it is so because every time we go through the highs of life, we know that we are alive. We go through the lows of life recalling the highs.

Belonging to a less-privileged African-American house, I grew up in an environment not different than yours. Where, late at night I would often hear suppressed sobs of mothers not having an answer for their children why their dad had left. I witnessed heartaches and heartbreaks. There was a thought etched on my mind that no matter how hard I tried; I would never get the same job as a person from outside of the hood.

All the times I watched people fight in their lives, what used to leave me amazed was their courage. The people, who despite returning home defeated, would step out the next morning in the hopes of finding work. It was the hope that I saw in them daily that paved a path. I tailed it as it led me out of the hoods. I had no resources or access to help. What I had was the dream of getting out of hardships and making my life easy.

Every time I was pulled back, I reminded myself of my goal until one day I achieved it. But what happened next left me perplexed. I was out of the hoods. I was living a life I dreamt of. Then why I felt something was amiss after some time? It was confusing. At times, I felt I was ungrateful. The beginning of my journey was hard, but I made it easy. So, why was the end feeling out of place? I was unable to find an answer until one day I found myself doing something that cost me nothing but was far more rewarding than having to work as an entrepreneur.

I managed to help someone overcome a certain setback in their life with barely my presence and a set of words. The feeling was similar to what I felt when I was embarking on my journey to achieve my goals. That was the exact moment in life when I understood what people meant when they used to say that each ending is a new beginning and life goes on. Without a beginning, there would be no learning. It was learning that made me want to go beyond my reach until I fulfilled my dreams. Learning is the best of wealth any person can have.

After having stepped out from my comfort zone and risking everything I ever knew, I managed to start a business of my own. Once that was successful, I fell in a transitionary period and found it to be the least amusing time of my life. During those days, my heart started to skip a beat. I knew I had to do something more again. Then I turned back in my life and saw how there were many people willing to follow my footsteps. I knew I had to help them because to see them in pain reminded me of the times I was in pain.

"Now, this is not the end. It is not even the beginning of the end. But it is, perhaps, the end of the beginning."

- Winston Churchill

I understood that after my journey of struggles came to an end, it was time for me to set new goals. Similarly, right now, your life may seem like it can never get better. That you will be stereotyped till the end of time for your color, for your background, and for not having a complete family as per the society's acceptance. You might get a degree, but it will never be enough. All of these doubts will prevail and cloud your mind. But the day this happens, the day when all these cynical thoughts fog your senses, know it is the time for those problems to end and for a new journey to begin.

If others can change their lives, then so can you. All you need do is know how to reach your potential. Tell yourself that you are strong, make a plan, and put it up in front of you. At the end of each day, reflect on the efforts you did to be where you are. Every day when you reflect, it will prepare you for the beginning of tomorrow. This is life. Every day the sun sets to allow for the end and then it rises back again, signifying a new beginning. Then why should you stop at just one thing in life?

Set up goals for yourself throughout life and you will see that life is not all that bad. Start small and from completing your education. Move on to the next set of goals. It could be trying to secure a job or trying to start your business. Make a smaller set of goals for these bigger ones. One after another, as you achieve them, you will feel a surge of belief within you. That belief will light up your heart. And remember, if you share this light, it won't lessen, it will only grow.

Just because you have succeeded once, it isn't the end of your journey. It is important to find the next goal, which is the new beginning. After achieving a goal, you must embark on a new one. Keep striving for greatness because there is no end to growth and success. Start a new journey of your own, as I have, and let it be the source of guidance for those suffering alone in the hoods.

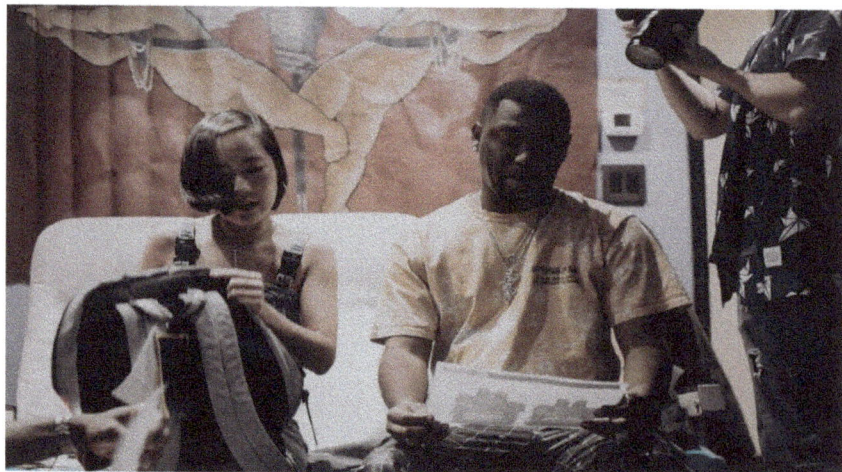